THIS BOOK BELONGS TO:

Published in the United States by Clarkson Potter/Publishers, an imprint of Random House, a division of Penguin Random House LLC, New York.
clarksonpotter.com

Clarkson Potter is a trademark and Potter with colophon is a registered trademark of Penguin Random House LLC.

ISBN 978-1-9848-2467-7

Printed in China

Cover and interior design by Caitlin Metz

1 3 5 7 9 10 8 6 4 2

First Edition

TO OUR INNER CHILDREN, TRIANGLE AND BLOBBY,
ALL OF THIS IS FOR YOU. THANK YOU FOR KEEPING US SAFE.

WE GOT YOU NOW.

THIS BOOK IS MEANT TO BE A CONVERSATION; WITHOUT YOU IT'S ONLY HALF WRITTEN.

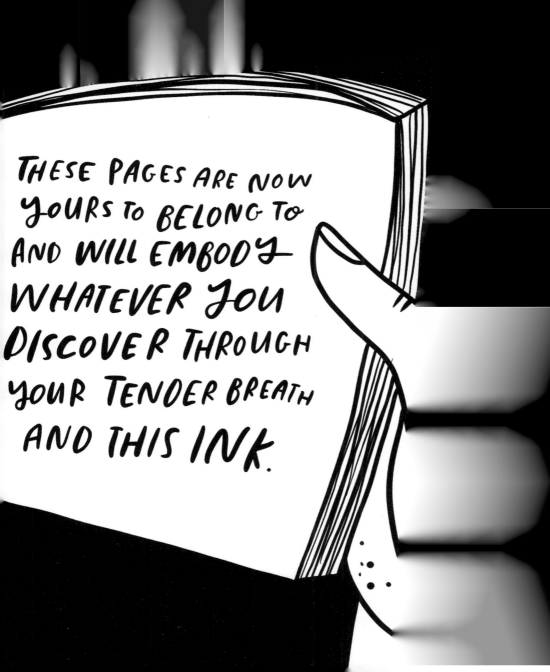

THERE ARE NO LIMITS TO WHAT YOU CAN DO WITHIN THIS BOOK; WRITE ALL OVER IT, FOLD DOWN THE CORNERS, OR TEAR OUT ITS PAGES TO FRAME.

USE IT AS A GUIDE, AN AWAKENING, OR A VIGOROUS CALL TO ACTION. READ IT AS A POEM, A MANIFESTO, OR A UNIVERSAL MEMOIR. LET IT HOLD YOUR SECRETS AND ABSORB YOUR TEARS, FREE AND UNFILTERED.

AS YOU GROW HELD BY THESE PAGES, REMEMBER YOUR BODY IS a VAST TERRAIN of UNIQUE COMPLEXITIES. THIS JOURNEY ISN'T MEANT TO BE EFFORTLESS NOR CONSUMED IN ONE PASS; IT BEGINS AT THE INTERSECTIONS of RESISTANCE AND TRANSFORMATION, INTIMACY AND RECLAMATION, TRUST AND REBIRTH.

COMING HOME TO YOURSELF IS A LIFELONG PRACTICE, FOR YOU ARE ALWAYS ARRIVING, ALWAYS RESETTLING INTO INFINITE SPACE.

MAY THIS BOOK
BE A REFUGE TO ALL
THAT YOU ARE AND
CONTINUE TO BECOME

GLOSSARY of FREQUENTLY USED WORDS WITHIN THIS BOOK

HOME
A SPACE THAT PROVIDES REFUGE, COMFORT, AND BELONGING.

EMBODIMENT
INHABITING YOUR BODY AND SENSES, AND BEING PRESENT WITH ALL of YOU.

BODY
A CONTAINER, A BOOK, YOUR HOME.

DISEMBODIMENT
THE STATE of DISASSOCIATION FROM THE BODY AND SENSES, a LACK of INTEGRATION BETWEEN THE MIND AND THE BODY.

TRAUMA
A PROFOUNDLY DISTRESSING EXPERIENCE THAT THREATENS YOUR SAFETY AND/or SENSE of SELF AND HAS AN ADVERSE IMPACT ON YOUR LIFE.

INNER CHILD
ALL THE VERSIONS of YOUR YOUNGER SELF THAT LIVE WITHIN YOU.

LINEAGE
THE WHISPERS IN YOUR DNA, YOUR HISTORY, AND EVERY PERSON WHO CAME BEFORE YOU.

RECLAMATION
THE PRACTICE of DECOLONIZING* THE BODY AND TAKING BACK WHAT'S YOURS.

RESILIENCE
THE ABILITY TO COPE WITH ADVERSITY, ADAPT TO CHALLENGES, AND/or CHANGE IN SUSTAINABLE AND NOURISHING WAYS.

SELF-SOOTHING

THE PROCESS of CALMING YOURSELF DOWN IN MOMENTS of DISTRESS.

SELF-REGULATING

A PROACTIVE PROCESS of TAKING CARE of YOURSELF TO STAY BALANCED PHYSICALLY, MENTALLY, AND EMOTIONALLY.

SELF-ACCEPTANCE

A NONLINEAR AND IMPERFECT PRACTICE of HOLDING WHO YOU'VE BEEN, WHO YOU ARE, AND WHO YOU WILL BECOME WITH EQUAL TENDERNESS AND CARE.

HEALING

THE RADICAL AND NON-LINEAR QUEST of COMING HOME TO YOURSELF. A RESTORATION of THE PHYSICAL, EMOTIONAL, AND SPIRITUAL PARTS of YOURSELF.

SELF-KEEPING

THE RADICAL ACT of BECOMING A NURTURING AND SUPPORTIVE CONTAINER FOR YOURSELF THROUGH SUSTAINABLE PRACTICES THAT BUILD RESILIENCY.

INTUITIVE MOVEMENT

FREE-FLOWING MOVEMENT, DONE WITHOUT PERFORMATIVE INTENT. WHEN YOU LET YOUR BODY SPEAK.

GROUNDING

CONNECTING TO YOUR CENTER on THE EARTH BY USING YOUR SENSES.

* DECOLONIZE

AN ACTIVE AND RADICAL RESISTANCE TO THE EXPLOITATION AND AUTHORITY OVER BODIES BY OPPRESSIVE SYSTEMS of POWER.

BELONGING

CULTIVATING A DEEP CONNECTION TO THE HUMAN COLLECTIVE WHILE ALLOWING YOURSELF TO BE SEEN IN ALL YOUR IMPERFECTIONS.

SECTION ONE
HOME + BODY

YOUR BODY IS A SQUISHY LIVING CREATURE ON A SPINNING ROCK IN SPACE

IT IS A LOST AND FOUND FOR STARDUST, & HOME TO WHAT MAKES you HUMAN. IT IS A SEEKER of TRUTH, WHERE THE SPACE BETWEEN WONDERING WHY YOU'RE HERE AND WHERE YOU'LL GO IS THE MEANING of LIFE. YOUR BODY IS WHERE YOU PROCESS EXISTENCE, AND TASTE THE SALT of YOUR TEARS. IT IS & SOFT COLLECTION of MOMENTS, TRAUMAS, MEMORIES, AND BELIEFS. YOUR BODY IS A HOME TO EVERYONE WHO CAME BEFORE YOU, WHERE YOUR MOTHER'S HANDS AND YOUR GREAT-GRANDFATHER'S LAUGH BECOME YOUR OWN.

IT IS THE UNIVERSE PERFORMING ITSELF; WILD, SACRED, AND FED BY TREES. IT IS THE BEGINNING AND END TO EACH DAY.

YOUR BODY IS & MIRACLE

AN INEXHAUSTIBLE LIST of WHAT a BODY CAN BE

BODY of WATER
THE BODY IS MADE UP of MOSTLY WATER.

A CANVAS
YOUR BODY IS A CANVAS MARKED BY LAYERS of EXPLORATION; YOU ARE STROKES UPON STROKES of AWE.

ENERGY
AS YOU READ THIS, YOUR BODY IS PRODUCING 100 WATTS of POWER. YOU'RE BASICALLY A LIGHTBULB.

A COLLECTION of PARTS
YOU EXIST AT THE INTERSECTIONS of YOUR IDENTITIES — THE TUNNELS DUG BETWEEN, AND LINES STRUNG ACROSS. YOU ARE YOU BECAUSE of YOUR VARIOUS, CONTRADICTING SELVES.

CELLS
RIGHT NOW, OVER 37 TRILLION CELLS ARE GIVING STRUCTURE TO YOUR BODY AND KEEPING YOU ALIVE.

TWO SETS of DNA COMING TOGETHER

HUMANS SHARE 99% of THE SAME DNA. HOW EXTRAORDINARY THAT YOU CARRY ALL of HUMANITY WITHIN YOU.

AN ANTHOLOGY of YOU

A BOOK
YOU ARE AN ENDLESS TEXT. YOUR BODY HOLDS THE HISTORIES + STORIES of YOUR LINEAGE.

FORCE of NATURE

THE WINDING PATTERNS of YOUR BLOOD VESSELS MIRROR THE PATTERNS of LIGHTNING, TREE ROOTS + RIVER DELTAS.

a SQUISHY VESSEL

A SOFT, TENDER, EVERY-SIZE-MATTERS PLACE FOR ALL THAT IS HUMAN TO GENTLY LAND.

GALAXY (STARDUST)

EVERY ATOM IN YOUR BODY IS CREATED FROM STARS THAT EXPLODED BILLIONS of YEARS AGO—MANY of THOSE STARS WERE BILLIONS of YEARS OLD THEMSELVES.

SPACE of CREATION

A PLACE WHERE HUMAN BEINGS ARE MADE.

PLEASURE and PAIN

YOUR BODY MEETS AT THE CROSSROADS of PLEASURE AND PAIN, ACTION AND APATHY, FEELING AND SENSATION.

CONTAINER

A SACRED SPACE THAT CONTAINS YOUR INNERMOST THOUGHTS, FEELINGS, MEMORIES, AND SECRETS.

BACTERIA

YOUR BODY CARRIES TEN TIMES MORE BACTERIAL CELLS THAN HUMAN CELLS. YOU'RE KIND of AN ALIEN, MORE BACTERIA THAN HUMAN, AND HOME TO TINY CREATURES.

WHAT ELSE CAN a BODY BE ?!

A BARRIER or SHIELD

YOUR SKIN PROTECTS YOUR INNER ORGANS, RIB CAGE, THE BEAT of YOUR HEART. YOUR SKULL GUARDS THE WORKINGS of YOUR BEAUTIFUL MIND—BOUNDARIES KEEP YOU WHOLE.

A HOME CAN BE
a DOOR WITH FOUR
WALLS AND a ROOF,
BUT IT DOESN'T
HAVE TO BE

HOME CAN BE a LOST WORLD WAITING TO BE DISCOVERED, WHERE GHOSTS of YOUR PAST MEET THE FUTURE of YOUR HEALING. HOME IS WHERE YOU SEEK REFUGE IN YOURSELF, WHERE YOU RETREAT TO FEEL SAFE AND UNDERSTOOD.

IN ORDER TO CONSTRUCT THIS NEW MEANING of WHAT a HOME IS AND SHOULD BE, WE HAVE TO ACKNOWLEDGE AND HOLD SPACE FOR THE WAYS IN WHICH WE MIGHT HAVE LEFT OUR HOMES or BODIES AS a MEANS of STAYING SAFE. WE MUST LEARN HOW TO RECONSTRUCT THE PLACES WE EXIST IN.

LET'S ESTABLISH a NEW MEANING of WHAT IT IS TO BE HOME

AN INEXHAUSTIBLE LIST of WHAT a HOME SHOULD BE

A NEST
A PLACE WHERE YOU FEEL SAFE TO SOFTEN, ARE NURTURED, AND RECEIVE CONSISTENCY.

A BASE
WHERE YOU ESTABLISH YOURSELF, LET YOUR FREAK FLAG FLY, AND HOLD YOUR GROUND.

REFUGE
A PLACE OF PROTECTION, SHELTER + CARE. WHERE YOU REGULATE, UNRAVEL, AND RETURN TO HEAL.

CENTER

A PLACE WHERE YOU FEEL WORTHY of LOVE AND BELONGING. WHERE THE HEART IS TENDER AND UNCONDITIONAL.

OPEN ARMS
WHERE YOU EXIST JUST AS YOU ARE. WHERE SHAME, JUDGMENT, AND CRITICISM ARE LEFT AT THE DOOR.

ACCESSIBLE

WHERE ALL BODIES ARE HONORED AND DIVERSITY IS THE ONLY WAY.

A RESTING PLACE
FOR YOUR HEART
↓

AN ENIGMA
A PLACE of MYSTERY
AND ALLURE. WHERE YOU
FEEL WILD, FREE + BOUNDLESS.

WHERE YOUR AFFECTIONS
ARE RECEIVED, YOUR
TEARS ARE HONORED,
AND SECRETS ARE KEPT.

AN ANCHOR

THE PLACE YOU FEEL
GROUNDED, ONE THAT
YOU CLAIM. WHERE YOU
FEEL ATTACHED AND
SUPPORTED.

a NATURAL WHERE
HABITAT YOU CAN
RETURN TO THE SOURCE of IT
ALL AND FEEL CONNECTED TO
THE OCEAN, TREES, DESERTS,
AND MOUNTAINS — THE EARTH.

INTIMATE
QUARTERS

WHERE VULNERABILITY
MEETS PASSION AND CONSENT.
A PLACE YOU FEEL HELD
AND PULLED CLOSE.

COMMUNITY

A PLACE
of FAMILIARITY AND
CONNECTION. WHERE
YOU SPEAK YOUR TRUTH
AND ARE HEARD.

Your body knows how to receive chemical messages between trillions of cells carrying out distinct functions through a network of fragile systems. How to distinguish one trillion scents like honeysuckle, smoke, and seaweed. How to derive meaning and contemplate its place in the universe. How to follow its truth when assigned an incompatible sex or gender. How to store a quadrillion bytes of information in its brain; approximately the entirety of the internet.

IT KNOWS HOW TO PROTECT ITSELF FROM DANGER THROUGH SURVIVAL MECHANISMS HUNDREDS of THOUSANDS of YEARS OLD. HOW TO STAND UP TO INJUSTICE AND CREATE A BETTER WORLD FOR OTHER BODIES. HOW TO ACCESS IMMENSE PLEASURE, UNMITIGATED PAIN, AND HEALING. HOW TO BE A HOME TO THE TRILLIONS of BACTERIA LIVING WITHIN AND AROUND IT. AND HOW TO LOVE WITH RECKLESS ABANDON BEYOND THE EDGES of THE EARTH.

YOUR BODY IS
MADE UP of NEARLY
7,000,000,000,000,000,000,000,000,000
ATOMS. THE SUN, MOON, AND EARTH
ARE MADE UP of THESE TOO.
EVERY STAR YOU WITNESS CONTAINS
CARBON, HYDROGEN, NITROGEN, AND OXYGEN.

YOUR TENDER BODY IS ALSO
MADE of THESE ELEMENTS.

YOU ARE MADE
of STARDUST.

WHEN YOU WISH UPON
THE GLIMMERING
NIGHT SKY,
IT'S REALLY YOURSELF
YOU ARE WHISPERING TO;
THE STARS ARE
JUST A MIRROR,
REFLECTING HOW
POWERFUL
YOU ARE.

YOU HOLD THE WHOLE
UNIVERSE INSIDE
of YOU.

AS BIG AND COSMIC AS WE ARE,
HOLDING THE ENTIRE UNIVERSE WITHIN
YOU IS a MONUMENTAL UNDERTAKING.
THE TRUTH IS WE LIVE ON A GIANT
ROCK, NEXT TO a GLOWING BALL of FIRE,
IN a SILENT VOID WE CALL SPACE.

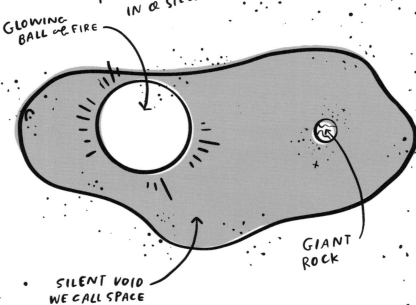

GLOWING
BALL of FIRE

GIANT
ROCK

SILENT VOID
WE CALL SPACE

WE SPEND OUR LIVES
NAVIGATING QUESTIONS MUCH TOO
VAST FOR US TO FULLY COMPREHEND,
LIKE WHY AM I HERE? WHO AM I?
WHAT'S THE MEANING of LIFE?
WHAT HAPPENS WHEN I DIE?

DESPITE
THE BRILLIANT
ENTANGLEMENT
of WARM BODIES
AND UNFATHOMABLE
BEAUTY of TEARS
AND TRIUMPH—
LIFE ON EARTH IS
ALSO A CRUEL,
PERPLEXING MESS

LIVING IN a WORLD
THAT OFTEN IGNORES,
DISCREDITS, AND AVOIDS
THE WONDER THAT IS YOU
MIGHT HAVE MADE INHABITING
YOURSELF INTOLERABLE, COUNTER-
INTUITIVE, or INACCESSIBLE TO YOU
AT TIMES or MAYBE EVEN
YOUR WHOLE LIFE.

THE DEPARTURE
FROM YOUR BODY (home)
MIGHT HAVE BEEN
VIOLENT or SUBTLE,
HAPPENING IN AN INSTANT
or ERODING OVER TIME.
YOU MAY HAVE NO
MEMORY of LEAVING
or IT MIGHT BE SEARED
INTO YOUR MIND.

EX. TRAUMA
or ABUSE

EX. CAPITALISM
or CULTURE

SHAME SPIRALS

CHILDHOOD TRAUMA

ABLEISM

CHRONIC ILLNESS

MENTAL ILLNESS

PTSD

RACIAL TRAUMA

SURVIVOR'S GUILT

FAT SHAMING

TRANSPHOBIA

DISPLACEMENT

LACK of HEALTH CARE, POVERTY

PURITY FEAR

CULTURE BEAUTY IDEALS

TRANSGENERATIONAL TRAUMA, CRITICISM

GENDER EXPRESSION DEATH of A LOVED ONE

SOCIETAL EXPECTATIONS

WE ARE OFTEN NAVIGATING HOW TO BECOME A SAFE LANDING FOR OURSELVES WHILE PROTECTING OUR BODY AGAINST THE THREAT of SYSTEMIC OPPRESSION, BROKEN CHILDHOODS, and CYCLES of TRAUMA.

SOMETIMES WE SHUT DOWN, NUMB OUT, REACT, and/or DETACH FROM REALITY To DEAL WITH THE OVERWHELM.

WHEN YOUR BODY HAS BEEN CONDITIONED TO PERCEIVE DANGER LONG AFTER IT'S GONE, IT CAN GET STUCK IN SURVIVAL PATTERNS THAT KEEP YOU ESTRANGED FROM YOURSELF.

FRUSTRATING AS IT MAY BE, IT'S IMPORTANT TO HONOR YOUR BODY FOR DOING WHAT IT KNEW BEST TO PROTECT YOU FROM HARM.

AS WE FIND SAFETY, CONNECTION, AND HEAL FROM OUR WOUNDS, THE BODY SLOWLY UNLEARNS ITS OLD DEFENSES and CREATES NEW PATTERNS of RESILIENCE THAT NURTURE US.

THIS IS THE WORK of COMING HOME TO YOURSELF.

UNDERSTANDING YOUR RESPONSE TO STRESS AND THREATENING SITUATIONS CAN HELP YOU MANAGE THEIR EFFECTS ON YOUR BODY.

YOU MAY IDENTIFY WITH ONE OR MORE OF THE FOLLOWING STRESS RESPONSES.

(YOUR PROTECTIVE CUES ARE JUST AS COMPLEX AS YOU ARE)

FIGHT

WHEN YOU PREPARE
TO CONFRONT AND
OVERCOME THE THREAT

FLIGHT

WHEN YOU ESCAPE THE
THREAT BY FLEEING,
EMOTIONALLY or PHYSICALLY

FREEZE

WHEN YOU SHUT DOWN
EMOTIONALLY or PHYSICALLY
AS AN ESCAPE

FAWN

WHEN YOU DE-ESCALATE
THE THREAT BY PLEASING OTHERS
TO MINIMIZE HARM DONE TO YOU

FIGHT

INTENSE ANGER or RAGE

URGE TO KICK, PUNCH, or THROW THINGS

BULLYING or SCARING PEOPLE

RAISED VOICE, SCREAMING, or FEELING LIKE EXPLODING

DEFENSIVE

REFUSAL TO ADMIT FAULT, EVEN WHEN WRONG

WHICH of THESE STRESS RESPONSES DO you IDENTIFY WITH?

RESTLESS, TRAPPED, LOOKING FOR A WAY OUT

LEAVING THE SITUATION

AVOIDING CONFRONTATION

FLIGHT

FINDING DISTRACTIONS FROM THE SITUATION

FIDGETING LIMBS

IGNORING or ACTING LIKE NOTHING EVER HAPPENED

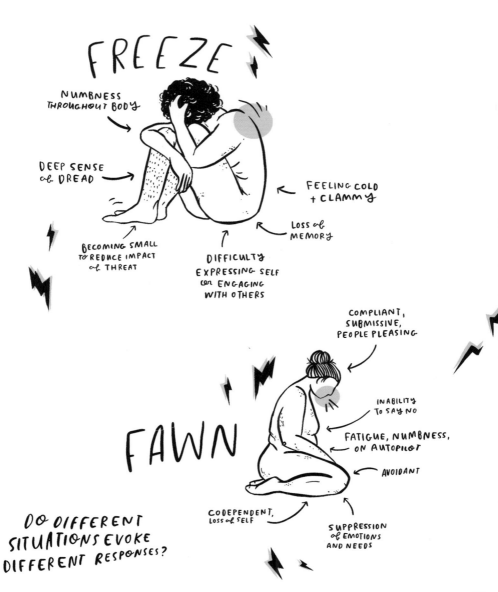

FREEZE

NUMBNESS THROUGHOUT BODY

DEEP SENSE of DREAD

FEELING COLD + CLAMMY

Loss of MEMORY

BECOMING SMALL To REDUCE IMPACT of THREAT

DIFFICULTY EXPRESSING SELF or ENGAGING WITH OTHERS

COMPLIANT, SUBMISSIVE, PEOPLE PLEASING

INABILITY To SAY NO

FAWN

FATIGUE, NUMBNESS, ON AUTOPILOT

AVOIDANT

CODEPENDENT, LOSS of SELF

SUPPRESSION of EMOTIONS AND NEEDS

DO DIFFERENT SITUATIONS EVOKE DIFFERENT RESPONSES?

YOU RETURN TO YOUR
BODY BY WAY of WHERE
YOU LEFT

THAT MEANS YOU ARE
FORCING YOURSELF THROUGH
FRACTURED SPACES
WHERE THE BROKEN BITS
MAKE JAGGED CUTS

FITTING YOUR
GROWN BODY INTO A SPACE
THAT PERHAPS HASN'T BEEN
INHABITED SINCE
CHILDHOOD REQUIRES

PATIENCE, TENDERNESS, AND FINESSE.

YOUR HOMECOMING
MAY BE OVERSHADOWED
BY DEMONS THAT HAVE NOT JUST
BEEN LURKING IN CLOSETS, BUT
HAVE BEEN DRINKING TEA IN THE DINING
ROOM AND SLEEPING IN YOUR BED.

IT MAY FEEL LIKE
YOU ARE THE INTRUDER,
BECAUSE THEY LIVE
HERE NOW.

THE THING TO REMEMBER
IS THAT YOU'RE HERE BECAUSE
SOME PART of YOU IS SAFE
ENOUGH TO FEEL.

THE MORE YOU FEEL, THE
MORE IT HURTS.
IT'LL HURT AND HURT
AND YOU'LL FEEL AFRAID
BECAUSE WHEN IT FELT
LIKE THIS BEFORE, YOU WERE
ALONE AND IT WAS VERY DARK.

BUT IT'S NOT THEN. IT'S NOW,

AND ALL THE THINGS THAT MADE YOU FEEL SAFE ENOUGH TO FEEL ARE HERE TO CARRY YOU THROUGH.

SECTION TWO

BELONGING

INNER PARTS

LINEAGE

PLACES

THE EARTH

SHADOW SELF

OTHER BEINGS

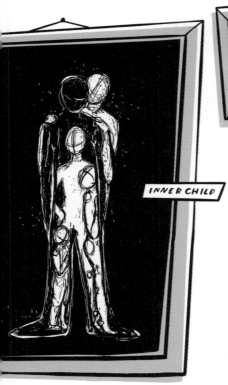

INNER CHILD

ALL THAT EXISTS WITHIN US, OUR MANY PARTS AND INTRICATE SELVES,

WHO WE ARE, AND WHAT WE DO IS POWERED BY THE STORIES WE TELL OURSELVES, BASED ON THE BELIEFS THEY'RE ROOTED IN.

OUR BELIEF SYSTEMS ARE INGRAINED WITH MESSAGES FROM OUR CHILDHOOD, FAMILY, RELIGION, EDUCATION, SOCIETY, AND SOCIAL NORMS.

AN INEXHAUSTIBLE
LIST of THINGS you
BELONG TO

LINEAGE
YOU CARRY ALL WHO CAME BEFORE YOU WITHIN YOUR BONES.

INNER PARTS
YOU ARE MULTIPLICITOUS, a COMMUNITY of UNIQUE AND INTERJECTING VOICES.

GRIEF

ANXIETY

SILLINESS

INNER CHILD
YOU ARE AT ONCE, EVERY AGE YOU'VE EVER BEEN.

SHADOW SELF

THE PARTS YOU WANT TO HIDE AWAY AND PRETEND DON'T EXIST.

THE EARTH

YOUR TRUE HOME AND MOST SACRED CONNECTION TO ALL THAT THERE IS.

OTHER BEINGS

HUMAN CONNECTION IS THE FOUNDATION of EXISTENCE. WE CANNOT DO THIS ALONE.

PLACES

FROM YOUR GRANDMOTHER'S HOUSE TO YOUR FAVORITE PARK, YOU BELONG TO THE SPACES THAT MAKE YOU FEEL AT HOME.

YOUR BODY CONTAINS MANY STORIES, BUT NOT ALL OF THEM WERE WRITTEN BY YOU
I AM NOT GOOD ENOUGH
THERE IS SOMETHING WRONG WITH ME
WHAT STORIES WERE WRITTEN WITHOUT YOUR PERMISSION?
I AM

"YOU LEARN FROM THE PART of THE STORY YOU FOCUS ON." —HANNAH GADSBY

HOW WILL YOU REWRITE THESE STORIES AND THEIR LIMITING BELIEFS?

'G IS
LT. IT'S
FAULT.
IS MY
LT. I AM NOT
OD ENOUGH.
UNLOVABLE.
THING
ME.

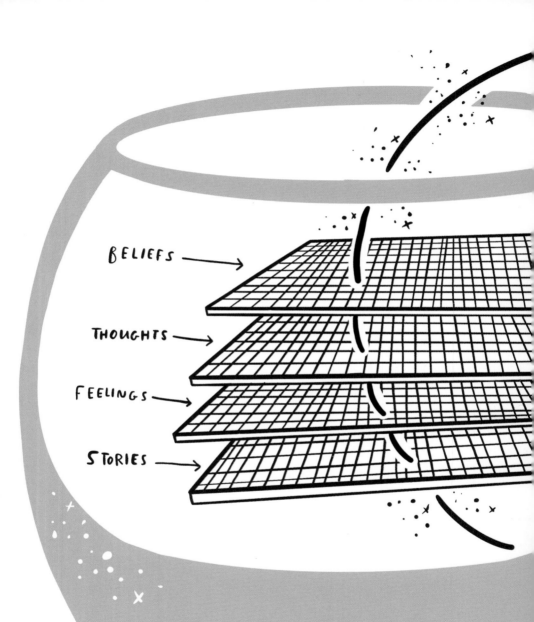

BELIEFS

THOUGHTS

FEELINGS

STORIES

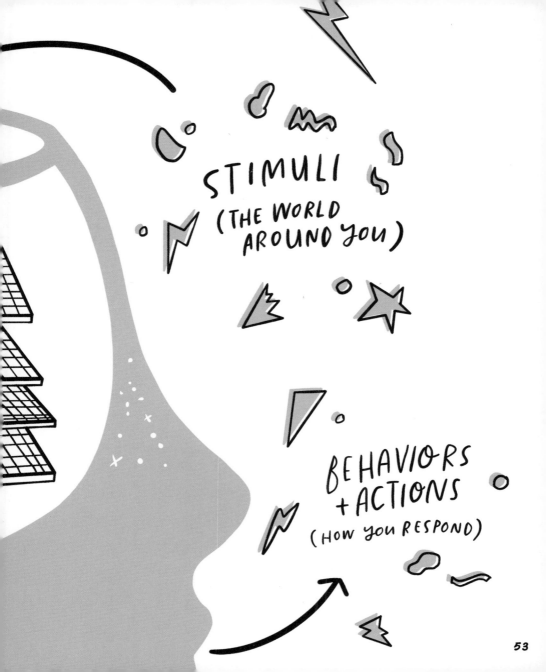

STIMULI
(THE WORLD AROUND YOU)

BEHAVIORS + ACTIONS
(HOW YOU RESPOND)

ALL THE THINGS

BELIEFS + STORIES

YOUR BELIEFS AND STORIES ACT
AS A FILTER, IMPACTING YOUR
SENSE of BELONGING

THE THINGS YOU
ALLOW THROUGH YOUR FILTER

IN ORDER TO SHIFT WHAT YOU THINK AND FEEL ABOUT YOURSELF, YOU MUST EXAMINE THE QUALITY + CHARACTERISTICS of YOUR FILTER.

TAKE ONE OR MORE of YOUR STRONGEST BELIEFS THROUGH THE FOLLOWING FLOW →

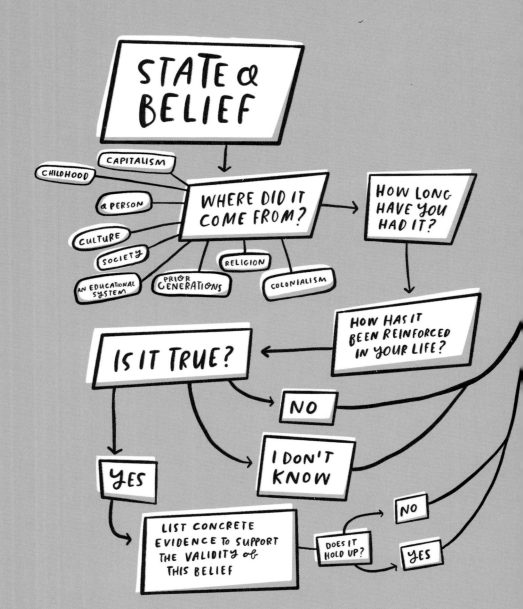

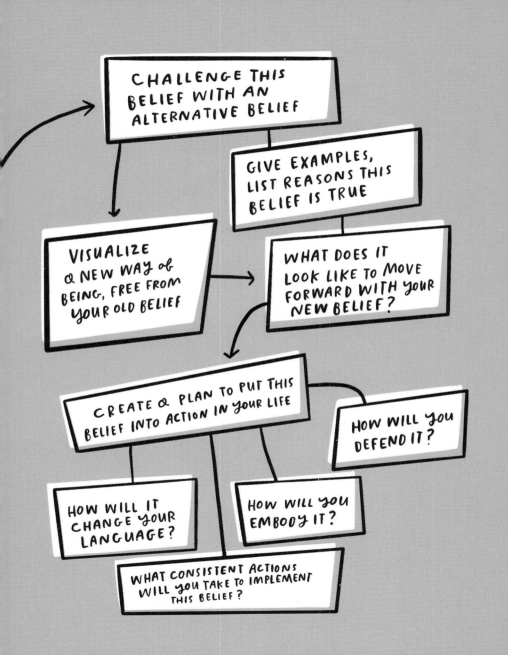

CHALLENGE THIS BELIEF WITH AN ALTERNATIVE BELIEF

GIVE EXAMPLES, LIST REASONS THIS BELIEF IS TRUE

VISUALIZE a NEW WAY of BEING, FREE FROM YOUR OLD BELIEF

WHAT DOES IT LOOK LIKE TO MOVE FORWARD WITH YOUR NEW BELIEF?

CREATE a PLAN TO PUT THIS BELIEF INTO ACTION IN YOUR LIFE

HOW WILL YOU DEFEND IT?

HOW WILL IT CHANGE YOUR LANGUAGE?

HOW WILL YOU EMBODY IT?

WHAT CONSISTENT ACTIONS WILL YOU TAKE TO IMPLEMENT THIS BELIEF?

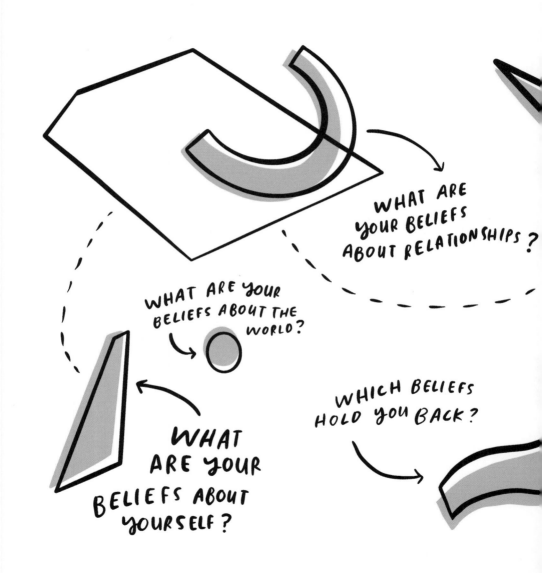

WHAT ARE YOUR BELIEFS ABOUT RELATIONSHIPS?

WHAT ARE YOUR BELIEFS ABOUT THE WORLD?

WHICH BELIEFS HOLD YOU BACK?

WHAT ARE YOUR BELIEFS ABOUT YOURSELF?

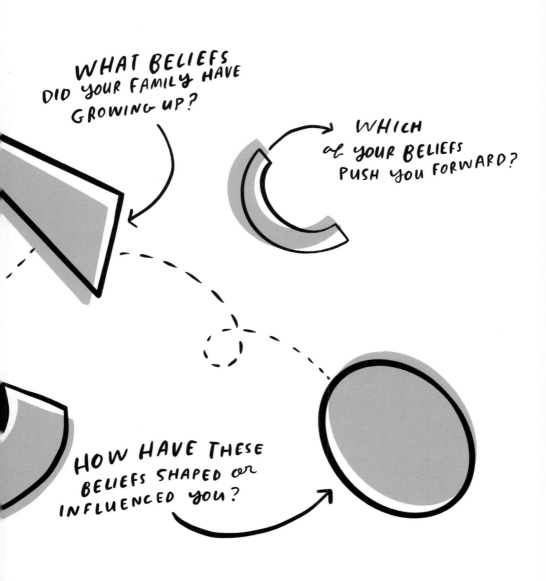

WHAT BELIEFS DID YOUR FAMILY HAVE GROWING UP?

WHICH of YOUR BELIEFS PUSH YOU FORWARD?

HOW HAVE THESE BELIEFS SHAPED or INFLUENCED you?

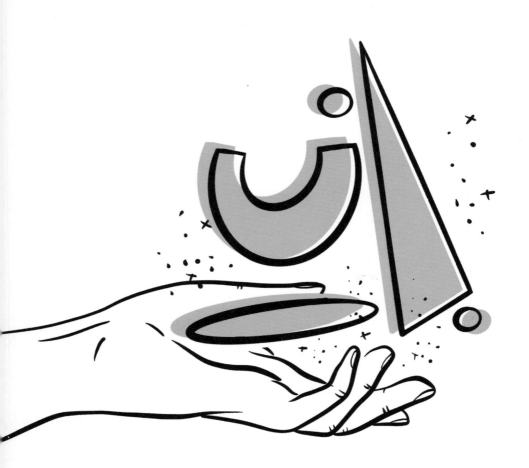

WHAT STORIES DO YOU LOVE ABOUT YOURSELF, YOUR BODY, AND THE WORLD?

WHAT ARE THE BELIEFS THAT DRIVE THESE STORIES?

HOW WILL YOU REWRITE THE STORY of YOUR BODY To CREATE A HOME FOR YOURSELF?

HOW DO THESE BELIEFS INFLUENCE YOUR SENSE of BELONGING?

WHAT WOULD HAPPEN IF YOU BELIEVED THAT YOU BELONG?

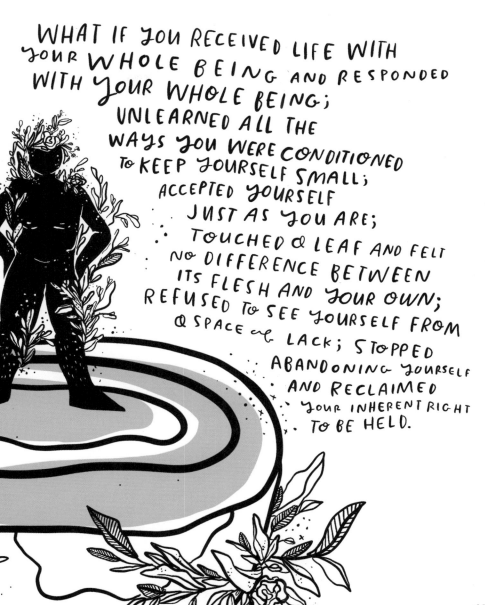

WHAT IF YOU RECEIVED LIFE WITH YOUR WHOLE BEING AND RESPONDED WITH YOUR WHOLE BEING; UNLEARNED ALL THE WAYS YOU WERE CONDITIONED TO KEEP YOURSELF SMALL; ACCEPTED YOURSELF JUST AS YOU ARE; TOUCHED A LEAF AND FELT NO DIFFERENCE BETWEEN ITS FLESH AND YOUR OWN; REFUSED TO SEE YOURSELF FROM A SPACE OF LACK; STOPPED ABANDONING YOURSELF AND RECLAIMED YOUR INHERENT RIGHT TO BE HELD.

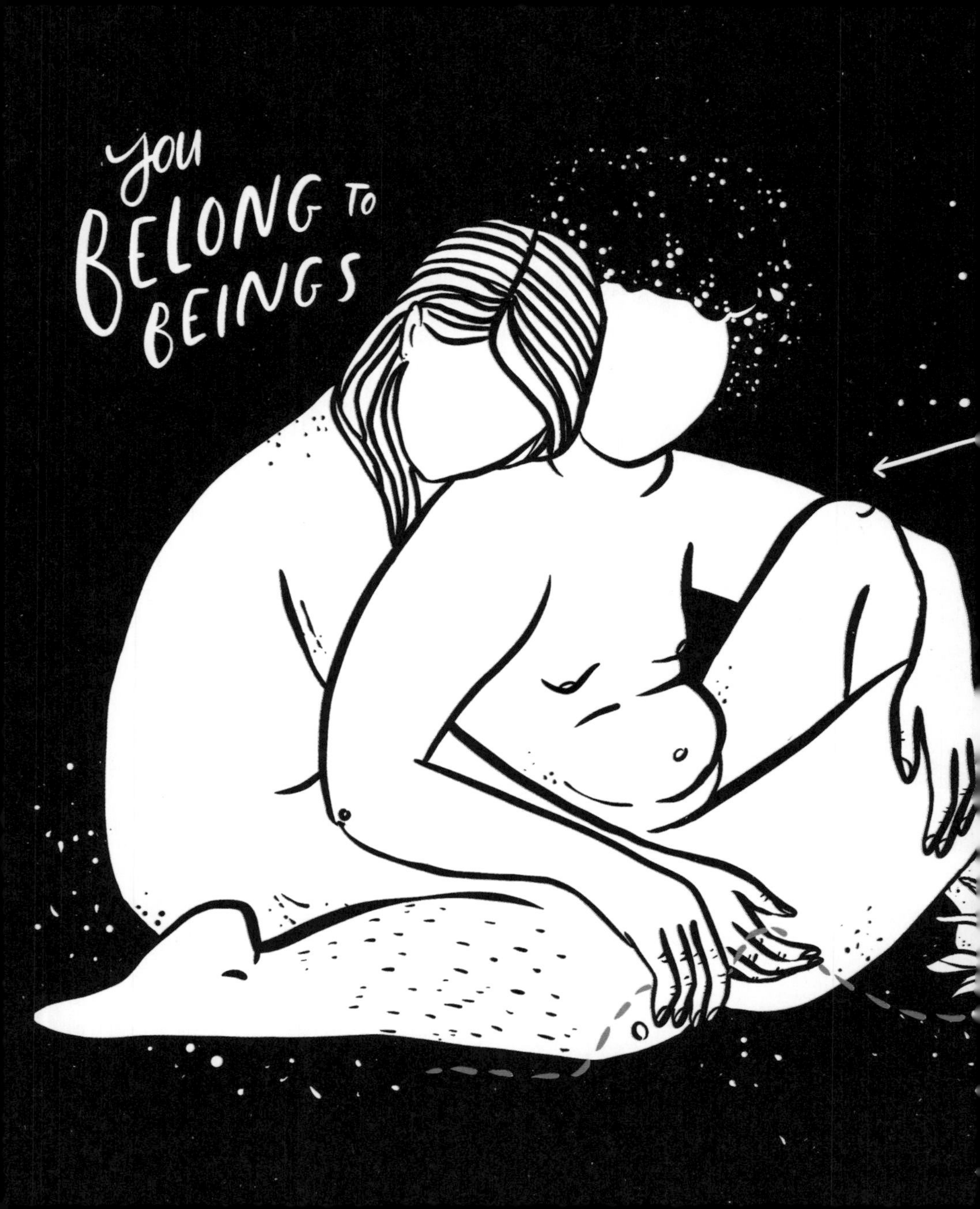
YOU
BELONG TO
BEINGS

WE BELONG TO ONE ANOTHER BY WAY of SHARING THE SAME PLANET, AND 99% of THE SAME DNA; WE ALL LONG, GRIEVE, CELEBRATE, AND TURN TO EACHOTHER TO SURVIVE.

EOPLE

PLANTS

PETS

WHO DO YOU BELONG TO?
WHO BELONGS TO YOU?

HOW CAN YOU DEEPEN
YOUR CONNECTION
TO THE BEINGS IN YOUR LIFE?

HOW DOES IT FEEL TO BELONG TO SO MANY OTHER BEINGS?

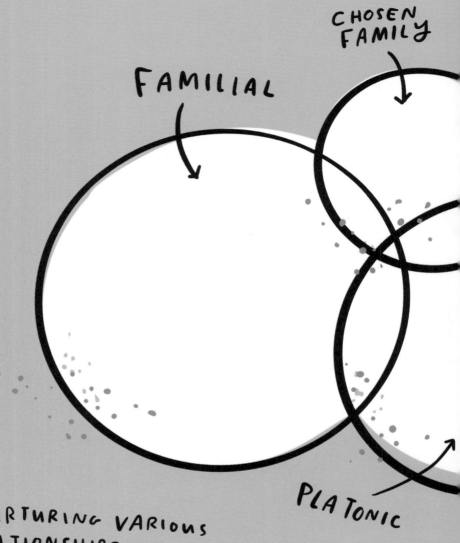

CHOSEN FAMILY

FAMILIAL

PLATONIC

NURTURING VARIOUS RELATIONSHIPS CAN BE HEALING FOR OUR DIFFERENT PARTS.

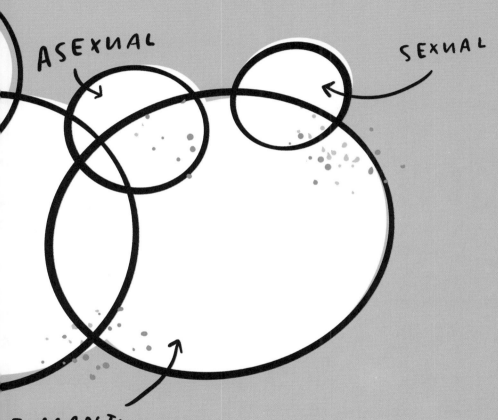

HOW ARE YOU NURTURING YOUR VARIOUS RELATIONSHIPS?

ASEXUAL

SEXUAL

ROMANTIC

BOUNDARIES HELP US RESTORE AND REBUILD A SENSE of SAFETY, TRUST, AND SELF-RESPECT.

No MORE

I WILL NOT

MY BODY FREEZES WHEN

I HATE

I FEEL UNCOMFORTABLE WHEN

I FEEL ANGRY AT

I FEEL DRAINED WHEN

BUT YOU CAN'T ESTABLISH BOUNDARIES UNTIL YOU TAKE INVENTORY of WHAT MAKES YOU FEEL UNSAFE, DISREGARDED, AND DRAINED. (FINISH THE FOLLOWING PHRASES TO BEGIN ESTABLISHING YOUR BOUNDARIES.)

I HAVE AN ISSUE WITH

IT'S NOT OKAY WHEN

I DON'T FEEL SAFE WHEN

I DON'T WANT TO

I CANNOT FREELY EXPRESS MYSELF WHEN

WHEN I'M UNSAFE MY BODY FEELS

IMAGINE ALL THE DIFFERENT KINDS of BOUNDARIES THAT COULD PROTECT YOU

a FORCE FIELD

CHAIN LINK

PERHAPS IT'S a THICK FOREST of PINE TREES or A LUMINESCENT FORCEFIELD THAT NO ONE CAN ENTER

THORNS

HEDGE

RAIL FENCE

CAGE

BRICK WALL

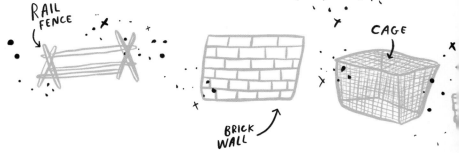

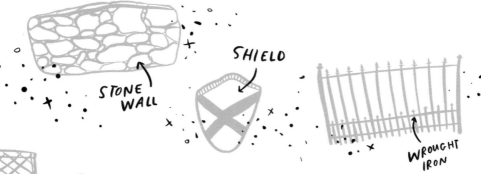

STONE WALL

SHIELD

WROUGHT IRON

CREATE a BOUNDARY FOR YOURSELF BY REFLECTING ON WHAT MAKES you FEEL SAFE — WHAT TASTES, SMELLS, SITES, SOUNDS, AND TEXTURES BRING you a SENSE of SECURITY AND EASE?

PICKET FENCE

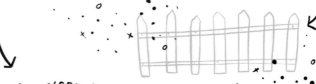

WHENEVER you NEED a SENSE of PROTECTION, KNOW THIS BOUNDARY IS ALWAYS WITHIN you. WHETHER IT'S RIGHT WHEN you WAKE UP, AT a FAMILY EVENT, OR DURING a STRESSFUL SITUATION, you CAN CALL ON IT ANYTIME.

PRIVACY FENCE

I LOVE IT WHEN

MY BODY SOFTENS WHEN

I FEEL SAFE WHEN

I WANT MORE

ONCE YOU'VE TAKEN INVENTORY of WHAT UNSETTLES AND DEPLETES YOU, IT'S EASIER TO IDENTIFY WHERE a BOUNDARY IS CROSSED, AND WHAT ACTION IS BEST TO BRING YOU PEACE AND PROTECTION.

WHERE DO THE BEINGS IN
YOUR LIFE BELONG IN THE
SPACE AROUND YOU?

↙ PEOPLE, PETS,
AND PLANTS

HOW DO YOU CREATE
SPACE + BOUNDARIES IN
TANDEM?

WHO HAS ACCESS TO
WHICH PARTS of YOU?

+ VARIOUS SELVES
or IDENTITIES
+ ENERGY | TIME
+ INTIMACY

HOW RIGID or
FLUID ARE THESE
GUIDELINES?

WE HAVE WITHSTOOD HUNDREDS of THOUSANDS of YEARS TOGETHER. OUR ABILITY TO SURVIVE AND THRIVE HAS ALWAYS BEEN DEPENDENT ON THE INEFFABLE BOND BETWEEN US. SUSTAINING AND NURTURING CONNECTIONS WITH OTHER BEINGS IS A WAY WE STAY CLOSE TO OUR SENSE of BELONGING.

TRY THIS MEDITATION WITH A FRIEND or LOVER

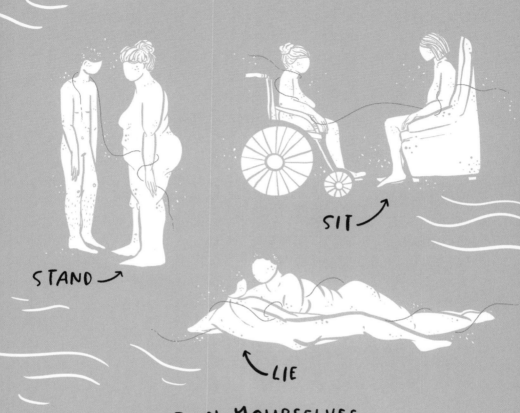

STAND →

SIT ↗

← LIE

POSITION YOURSELVES
ACROSS FROM EACH OTHER, IN
WHATEVER WAY FEELS
MOST COMFORTABLE.

GENTLY BRING YOUR FOREHEADS TOGETHER AT AN ANGLE THAT FEELS COMFORTABLE TO BOTH OF YOU, OR SIMPLY MAKE EYE CONTACT.

PLACE YOUR HANDS OVER EACH OTHER'S HEARTS.

WHEN YOU'RE SITUATED, BEGIN BY TAKING 5-10 BREATHS TOGETHER, INHALING AND EXHALING SIMULTANEOUSLY.

IF IT DOESN'T FEEL COMFORTABLE TO TAKE DEEP BREATHS, MEET YOUR BREATH WHEREVER IT IS, WITHOUT JUDGMENT.

TAKE YOUR TIME,

STAY IN THIS SPACE TOGETHER UNTIL YOUR BREATH SOFTENS,

UNTIL YOU FEEL READY TO PART.

RETURN TO THIS PRACTICE WHENEVER YOU NEED TO FEEL CONNECTED.

YOU BELONG TO THE EARTH

THE EARTH SERVES AS OUR TRUEST MIRROR BECAUSE IT'S THE MOST SYMBIOTIC RELATIONSHIP WE HAVE; EVERYTHING WE FEEL AND CREATE, THE EARTH REFLECTS.

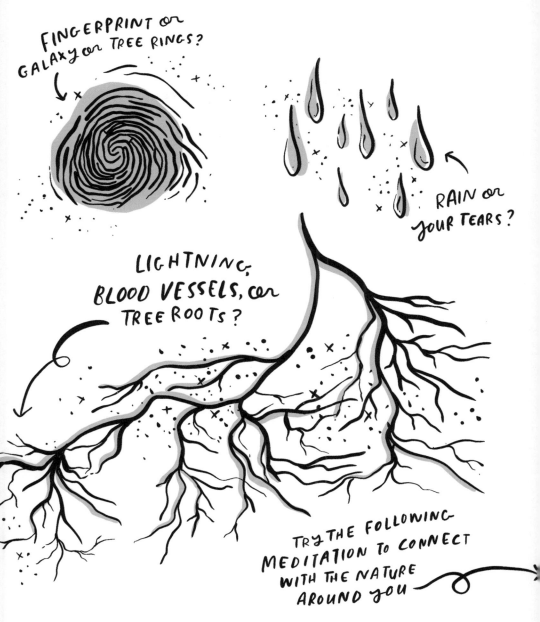

FINGERPRINT or GALAXY or TREE RINGS?

RAIN or YOUR TEARS?

LIGHTNING, BLOOD VESSELS, or TREE ROOTS?

TRY THE FOLLOWING MEDITATION TO CONNECT WITH THE NATURE AROUND YOU

GO OUTSIDE AND BEFRIEND A TREE. PLACE YOUR HAND OVER ITS BARK. LET YOUR ENERGIES MEET, AND NOTICE WHAT SENSATIONS OCCUR IN YOUR BODY.

BRING YOUR AWARENESS TO THE SYMBIOTIC CONNECTION BETWEEN YOU AND THE TREE. NOTICE HOW IT'S CREATING THE OXYGEN YOU'RE BREATHING IN, WHILE THE CARBON DIOXIDE YOU'RE EXHALING IS BEING USED AS ITS ENERGY.

SEE IF YOU CAN
FEEL THE RHYTHM
BETWEEN YOU AND
THE TREE—

EXCHANGING BREATH AND
NURTURING EACH OTHER'S
ABILITY TO SURVIVE.

TELL THE TREE A SECRET
or STORY. ASK FOR SUPPORT,
OFFER CARE IN RETURN.

AIR

BLOW BUBBLES

PRACTICE MINDFUL BREATHING

FLY A KITE

EARTH

PLANT A GARDEN

WALK BAREFOOT ON THE GROUND

PICK A WILD-FLOWER BOUQUET

CAN YOU CONNECT TO NATURE AROUND YOU BY ENGAGING WITH THE FOUR ELEMENTS?

FIRE

LIGHT CANDLES
DETOX IN A SAUNA
COOK SPICY FOOD
SUNBATHE

WATER

DRINK WATER
HAVE A GOOD CRY
GO SWIMMING
TAKE A BATH

Your
BODY IS THE
EARTH'S MIRACULOUS
HARVEST AND JUST LIKE ITS
DIVERSE ECOSYSTEMS,
YOU CONTAIN GRASSLANDS,
OCEANS, AND RAIN FORESTS
WITHIN YOU, ALL of WHICH
CREATE THE INFRASTRUCTURE
of WHO YOU ARE.

you BELONG to yourself

IT'S YOUR BIRTHRIGHT TO KNOW THAT YOU ARE ENOUGH WITHOUT SACRIFICING WHO YOU ARE. LET'S UNCOVER ALL THE WAYS YOU ALREADY BELONG

ALL THAT WE ARE IS A REMARKABLE COLLECTION of EVERY CHILD AND ADOLESCENT WE ONCE WERE AND CONTINUE TO EMBODY. HELPING YOUR INNER CHILD HEAL IS AN ESSENTIAL PART of RESTORING YOUR RELATIONSHIP TO YOUR SELF, AND HELPS REBUILD A FOUNDATION of SELF-COMPASSION AND TRUST.

a LIST of THINGS TODO
WITH YOUR INNER CHILD

☐ CLIMB A TREE

☐ FINGER PAINT

☐ MAKE A PLAYLIST TOGETHER

☐ TAKE THEM SHOPPING

☐ SWING

☐ LEARN A NEW SKILL TOGETHER

☐ WATCH CARTOONS

☐ PLAY DRESS UP

☐ BUILD A BLANKET FORT

☐ SLEEP WITH A STUFFED
    ANIMAL

☐ COLOR WITH CRAYONS

☐ DO A PUZZLE

☐ WRITE EACH OTHER LETTERS

RECONNECTING WITH a SENSE of PLAY AND CURIOSITY

TRANSFORMING BELIEFS DIGESTED FROM CHILDHOOD THAT HOLD YOU BACK

VALIDATING UNATTENDED WOUNDS AND HEALING THEM

REPARENTING YOURSELF

CULTIVATING DEEPER SELF-COMPASSION

YOUR INNER CHILD IS VULNERABLE AND MAY NEED TIME TO TRUST YOU.

CONTINUE ON GENTLY WITH YOURSELF.

HOLD A PHOTO of YOUR INNER CHILD (or SIMPLY CLOSE YOUR EYES AND IMAGINE THEM)

MEDITATE ON THE PHOTO or IMAGE IN YOUR HEAD. ASK THE CHILD INSIDE IF THEY WANT TO TELL YOU ANYTHING.

DON'T WORRY IF YOU DON'T FEEL AN IMMEDIATE CONNECTION; IF YOU CONTINUE THIS PRACTICE, a CONNECTION WILL GROW.

WRITE YOUR INNER CHILD A LETTER

THIS CAN BE A LETTER of APOLOGY, SUPPORT AND REASSURANCE, or SOMETHING LIGHTHEARTED. TAILOR IT TO THE NEEDS AND ENERGY of YOUR INNER CHILD.

DRAW YOUR INNER CHILD

MAKE THEM TANGIBLE BY DRAWING AND NAMING THEM. LET THEM GUIDE YOU, ASK THEM WHAT THEY WANT TO BE CALLED.

WRAP YOUR ARMS AROUND YOURSELF AND GIVE YOUR INNER CHILD A HUG, LET THEM KNOW YOU'RE HERE ⟶

THANKS FOR PROTECTING ME. I CAN TAKE CARE of US NOW
YOU ARE SAFE NOW
I'M LISTENIN
IT'S NOT YOUR FAULT
YOU ARE NOT ALONE
I'M SO SORRY
IT'S
YOU ARE LOVABLE
YOU ARE NOT ALONE
IT'S OKAY TO FEEL SAD
I WILL NEVER LEAVE YOU
I LOVE YOU

WE BELONG TO EACH OTHER
YOU ARE NOT ALONE
YOU ARE ENOUGH
YOUR NEEDS ARE VALID
YOU ARE NOT A FAILURE
I BELIEVE YOU
AY TO FEEL ANGRY
IT'S OKAY TO ASK FOR HELP
I WILL PROTECT YOU
IT'S OKAY TO SAY NO!
IT'S OKAY TO WANT HAPPINESS

You BELONG to ALL WHO CAME BEFORE YOU

YOU ARE AND FOREVER WILL BE AN ASTONISHING PATCHWORK of ALL THOSE WHO CAME BEFORE YOU AND CONTINUE TO EVOLVE FROM YOUR LINEAGE.

YOUR BODY CARRIES THEIR MEMORIES, EXPERIENCES, AND SURVIVAL WITHIN YOUR BONES. THE VOICES of YOUR ANCESTORS ARE WITHIN YOUR DREAMS.

GHOSTS WITHIN YOUR SHELL SERVE AS a REMINDER THAT YOU ARE NOT THE FIRST TO SUFFER, NOR TO LOVE, FOR THERE IS TOO MUCH LIFE INSIDE of YOU.

WHO CAME BEFORE YOU?

YOUR GREAT—GRANDFATHER'S WORK ETHIC _____

THE IMMIGRANTS WHO CHOSE TO EXPAND YOUR LINEAGE ON NEW SOIL _____

THE DREAMS of YOUR GREAT—GRANDMOTHER _____

THE FIRST SET of HOMO SAPIENS WHO EVOLVED INTO HUMANS MORE THAN 200,000 YEARS AGO _____

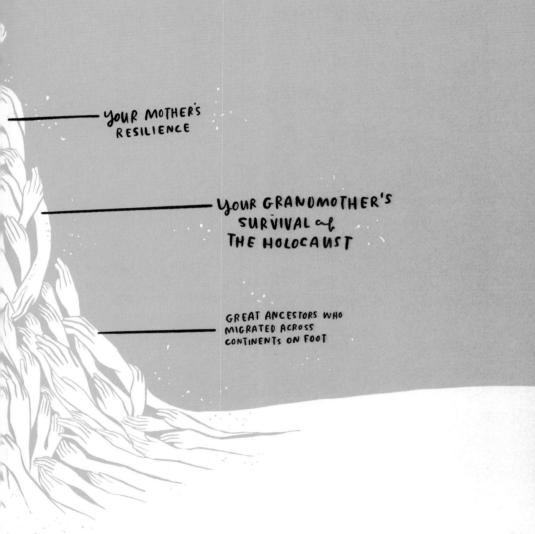

YOUR MOTHER'S
RESILIENCE

YOUR GRANDMOTHER'S
SURVIVAL of
THE HOLOCAUST

GREAT ANCESTORS WHO
MIGRATED ACROSS
CONTINENTS ON FOOT

THE WEIGHT of EVERY HUMAN'S GRIEF
THAT CAME BEFORE US LIVES IN OUR BLOOD.
EACH of US IS BORN FROM A LINEAGE of BODIES'
HISTORIES, AND PERSONAL NARRATIVES THAT ARE
CARRIED THROUGH OUR DNA AND INTO OUR
LIVED EXPERIENCE.

BY HEALING YOURSELF
YOU ARE HEALING THOSE WHO CAME
BEFORE YOU, ALL of WHICH PLAYS
A UNIQUE PART IN
HEALING THE WORLD.

THE DUTY WE HAVE AS
HUMANS TO UNLEARN AND TRANSFORM
WHAT WE'VE INHERITED TO MOVE OUR
SPECIES FORWARD IS A PROFOUND
RESPONSIBILITY.

YOU ARE NOT JUST HEALING
YOURSELF BUT THE WOUNDS of THOSE
WHOSE BODIES CONSPIRED TO
BRING YOU HERE.

REMEMBER THAT HEALING
TAKES TIME, MY LOVE.

IT'S A NON-
LINEAR JOURNEY THAT
MOVES IN MANY
DIRECTIONS

BECAUSE SOMETIMES MOVING
FORWARD ALSO MEANS TAKING
A FEW STEPS BACK

You're allowed to BREAK OPEN

You're allowed to let your wounds show

This is how the light finds you

you BELONG to your PARTS

YOU HAVE YOUR CORE SELF AND MANY COEXISTING PARTS of YOU SUCH as YOUR ANGRY, ABANDONED, FEARFUL, AND APATHETIC PARTS.

You ARE NOT JUST A "SELF" BUT A WHOLE MADE UP of MANY WORKING PARTS THAT CONTAIN DISTINCT NEEDS AND DESIRES. UNDERSTANDING AND BEFRIENDING OUR PARTS HELPS US NAVIGATE OUR EMOTIONAL LANDSCAPE WITH LESS OVERWHELM.

JUST LIKE you, THESE PARTS HAVE THEIR OWN EXPERIENCES AND NEEDS THAT INFLUENCE your THOUGHTS, FEELINGS, AND SENSE of THE WORLD.

WHEN UNDERSTANDING YOUR PARTS, IT'S IMPORTANT TO CONSIDER THAT YOUR ANGRY PART MIGHT NEED SOMETHING TOTALLY DIFFERENT FROM YOUR ANXIOUS PART WHEN ACTIVATED.

ANGRY

ANXIOUS

CAN YOU IDENTIFY
YOUR PARTS?

WHAT DO THEY NEED?

WHICH ONES ARE
MOST PRESENT FOR YOU?

WHEN WE FEEL an UNCOMFORTABLE EMOTION, WE OFTEN TRY TO DENY or PUSH IT AWAY. SOMETIMES FEELINGS ARE JUST FEELINGS AND THEY'RE NOT HERE TO DO ANYTHING MORE THAN PASS THROUGH you. IF WE GREET OUR EMOTIONS AS VISITORS AND ACKNOWLEDGE THEM, THEY START TO FEEL LESS OVERWHELMING.

NOTICE the EMOTIONS ARISING WITHIN YOU AND THE SENSATIONS THEY ARE CREATING IN YOUR BODY: HEAT, NUMBNESS, ACHING, ETC.

WITHOUT JUDGMENT, IDENTIFY THE EMOTION YOU'RE STRUGGLING WITH AND CONSIDER NAMING IT. IF IT FEELS COMFORTABLE, PLACE YOUR HAND OVER YOUR HEART FOR SUPPORT.

LIKE a VISITOR EXPLORING YOUR BODY— ONE THAT WILL EVENTUALLY LEAVE — NOTICE HOW THIS EMOTION IS a PART of YOU BUT DOESN'T DEFINE YOU.

EXPERIENCE YOUR EMOTION LIKE a WAVE ROLLING THROUGH THE SEA. NOTICE HOW YOU CAN'T STOP THE WAVE or CHANGE ITS DIRECTION, BUT YOU CAN RIDE IT OUT UNTIL IT PASSES.

GIVE YOURSELF SPACE TO BE PRESENT WITH THIS EMOTION. THE GOAL IS NOT TO JUDGE, CHANGE, or CONTROL IT.

JUST AS THE WAVES of A STORMY SEA EVENTUALLY CALM DOWN, SO WILL YOU. BEING HUMXN IS CHALLENGING, AND NO MATTER WHAT THAT VOICE IN YOUR HEAD SAYS, YOU ARE ENOUGH.

TAKE A MOMENT TO REFLECT ON A TIME YOU WORKED THROUGH THIS EMOTION. YOU MAY ALSO FOCUS ON A POSITIVE EXPERIENCE or GO TO A SAFE SPACE IN YOUR MIND: YOUR GARDEN, A MOUNTAIN, THE MOON.

AS YOU GENTLY ACCEPT AND NOT SHAME THE EMOTION, ALLOW THE WAVES TO CONTINUE ROLLING WHILE REMINDING YOURSELF THE STORM WILL PASS. IF IT FEELS SAFE, TAKE A FEW MINDFUL BREATHS, LETTING OUT A SIGH.

WHEN YOU'RE READY, THANK YOURSELF FOR SHOWING UP AND NURTURING YOUR HEART.

EVERYTHING
YOU FEEL IS
VALID + REAL
BUT THAT DOESN'T
MAKE IT TRUE

IT'S OKAY TO
FEEL YOUR FEELINGS
AVOID JUDGMENTS
of "GOOD" or "BAD"
VALIDATE YOUR FEELINGS
WITH COMPASSION
NAME THEM TO MAKE
THEM TANGIBLE—
DO NOT BUILD a DAM,
LET THEM FLOW →

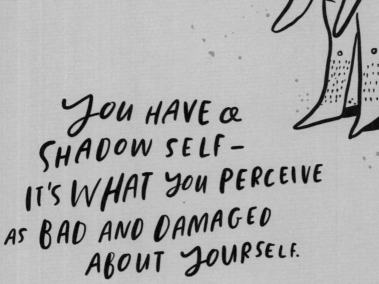

You HAVE a
SHADOW SELF —
IT'S WHAT You PERCEIVE
AS BAD AND DAMAGED
ABOUT YOURSELF.

IT'S A PART of US THAT WE REJECT AND KEEP HIDDEN.

WE CANNOT BURY OUR SHADOWS WITHOUT THEM UNCONSCIOUSLY MANIFESTING THROUGH OUR BELIEFS, BEHAVIORS, AND PROJECTIONS. IF WE CANNOT ACCEPT OUR DARK SIDE, WE WILL NEVER WITNESS THE BRIGHTNESS of OUR LIFE.

TRY to IDENTIFY YOUR SHADOW SELF BY RESPONDING TO THE FOLLOWING PROMPTS:

HOW WERE YOUR EMOTIONS REGULATED AS A CHILD?

WHAT EMOTIONS DO YOU TRY TO AVOID AS AN ADULT?

ARE YOU AFRAID of GOOD THINGS HAPPENING?

CAN YOU SHOW YOUR SHADOW SELF COMPASSION? →

MANY of THE FEELINGS AND BEHAVIORS OUR SHADOW SELF ELICITS IN US ARE MESSENGERS FROM OUR WOUNDS AND FEARS.

"NOTHING EVER GOES AWAY UNTIL IT HAS TAUGHT US WHAT WE NEED TO KNOW"

— PEMA CHÖDRÖN

PLEASURE, RAGE, LIBERATION, TINGLING, AND ACHING ARE ALL FELT EXPERIENCES IN THE BODY; YOUR BODY IS A PROCESS, NOT A STATIC BEING, AND IT MOVES WITH THE UNIVERSE.

YOU BELONG TO YOUR BODY

ELECTRIC QUEASY

ENERGIZED

FULL

free

FLUID HEAVY

NUMB SP

BUZZING TENSE

TENDER

PULSING

FLOATING

FROZEN

RELAXED

ACIOUS

SWEATY

FUZZY

RAW TINGLING

SOFT

ACTIVATED

ACHING

WHAT SENSATIONS ARE COMING UP IN YOUR HEAD?

WHAT TYPE of THOUGHTS ARE YOU HAVING TODAY?

HOW'S YOUR HEART TODAY?

WHAT FEELINGS ARE PRESENT IN YOUR CHEST?

WHAT DO YOU NOTICE IN YOUR NECK AND SHOULDERS?

WHAT SENSATIONS DO YOU NOTICE IN YOUR TUMMY TODAY?

WHAT ARE YOU HOLDING? WHAT IS WEIGHING ON YOU?

DO YOUR ARMS FEEL HEAVY or LIGHT?

WHAT DO YOU NOTICE IN YOUR THIGHS? HOW DO YOU FEEL ABOUT THEM? CAN YOU TELL THEM SOMETHING NICE?

GIVE YOUR HANDS a LITTLE SQUEEZE or GENTLE RUB.

HOW ARE YOUR LEGS? ARE THEY TIGHT? CAN YOU RELAX THEM FULLY?

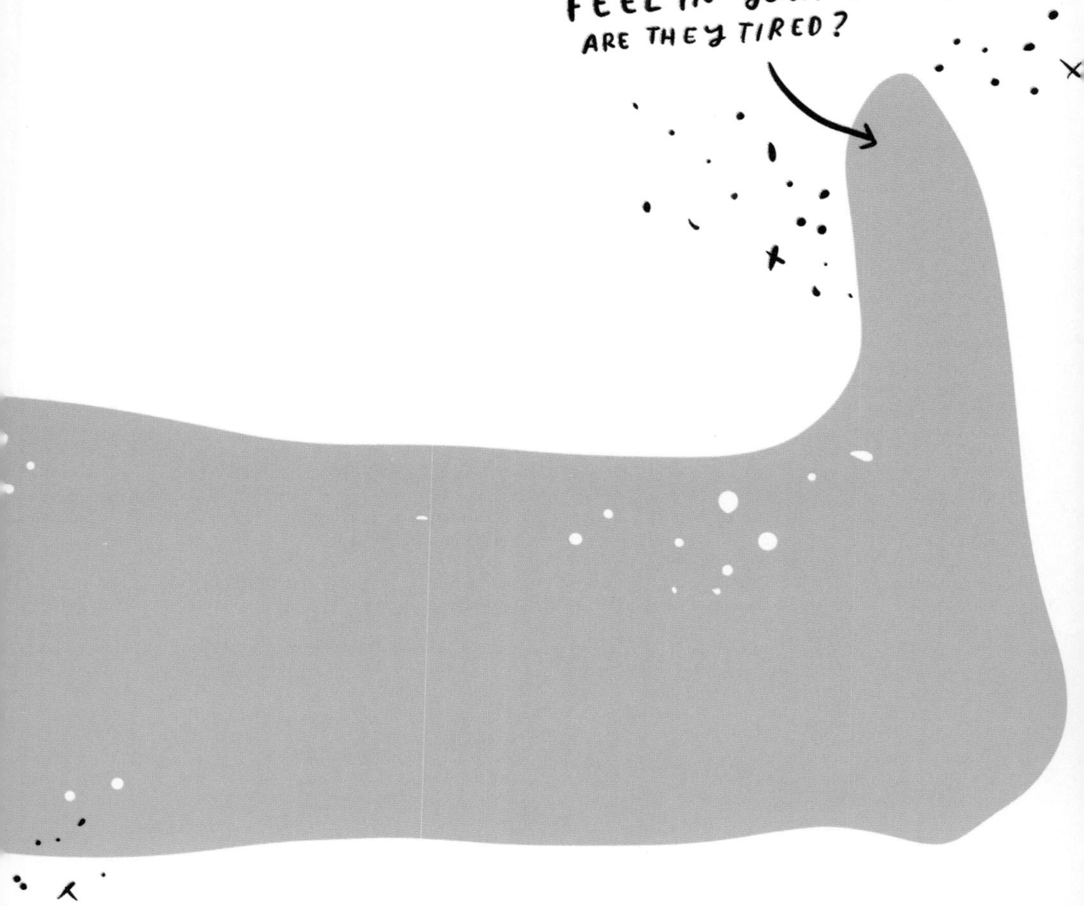
WHAT DO YOU FEEL IN YOUR FEET?
ARE THEY TIRED?

ONE VITAL WAY
WE CAN LEARN to
RESPOND to EXPERIENCes
IN OUR LIVES WITHOUT
SPIRALING INTO OLD DEFENSES
IS BY ACCESSING THE WISDOM of
OUR VAGUS NERVE

IT'S a MAGICAL NERVE THAT TRAVELS THROUGH YOUR BODY AND ESTABLISHES a NETWORK of INFORMATION WITH YOUR BRAIN, GUT, AND EVERY ORGAN YOU HAVE

WHEN YOU TRUST YOUR GUT or FEEL a STRONG SENSE of INTUITION, YOU CAN THANK YOUR VAGUS NERVE FOR THAT.

THE VAGUS IS A KEY PLAYER IN HELPING YOUR MIND AND BODY FIND BALANCE, BUT JUST LIKE A MUSCLE, IT NEEDS STRENGTHENING →

WAYS TO STRENGTHEN YOUR VAGUS NERVE

BREATHE, SLOW + DEEP

REST! RELAX!

GARGLE WATER

TAKE PROBIOTICS

PRACTICE MINDFUL MOVEMENT

SPLASH COLD WATER ON YOUR FACE

SING! HUM! CHANT!

GET Q MASSAGE

ENGAGE IN DEEP + MEANINGFUL HUMAN CONNECTION

(HUG, LAUGH, HOLD HANDS)

* LEARN MORE ABOUT THE VAGUS NERVE BY READING STEPHEN PORGES'S POLYVAGAL THEORY

ACTIVATING YOUR VAGUS NERVE
RELEASES a MYRIAD of SPECIAL
CHEMICALS THROUGHOUT YOUR BODY,
CREATING a RELAXATION RESPONSE,
EASING ANXIETY, AND SOOTHING
THE NERVOUS SYSTEM.

THE VAGUS IS RESPONSIBLE FOR
DIGESTION, REST, AND RESTORATION,
WHICH IS THE OPPOSITE RESPONSE
TO BEING IN a STATE of FIGHT,
FLIGHT, FREEZE, or FAWN.

SO THE MORE WE STRENGTHEN OUR VAGUS NERVE, THE MORE WE'RE ABLE TO MAKE OUR BODIES FEEL LIKE HOME.

SHIFTING OUR RESPONSE TO THREAT TAKES TIME, COMPASSION, AND HEALING THE NERVOUS SYSTEM UNTIL WE ARE MORE PRONE TO FACE + REGULATE THAN FIGHT, FLIGHT, FREEZE, OR FAWN.

FACE AND REGULATE

WHEN YOU DEAL WITH MATTERS DIRECTLY, ASSERT YOUR NEEDS, ESTABLISH BOUNDARIES, AND SELF-REGULATE.

COMMUNICATES PERSONAL NEEDS

CONFRONTS ISSUES DIRECTLY

SELF-REGULATES TO RE-CREATE BALANCE

MAINTAINS BOUNDARIES

DEAREST HUMAN,
AS YOU CONTINUE
THIS WILD AND WONDROUS
RIDE IN YOUR BODY, MAY
YOU ALWAYS RETURN
HOME TO YOURSELF, AND
FEEL THE INCREDIBLE
POWER WITHIN YOU AS
A REMINDER of HOW VAST
YOU ARE

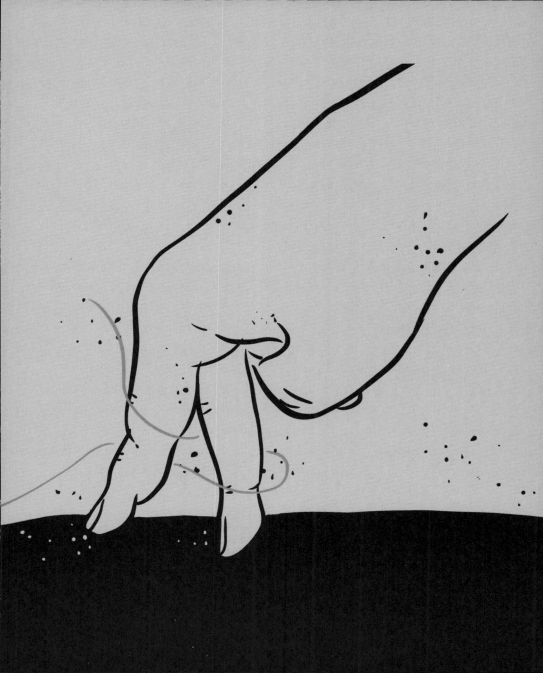

THE UNIVERSE
CHOSE YOUR
BODY AS a HOME
FOR ITSELF,

a HOME
FOR YOUR DEEPEST
EXPRESSION AND
DANCE WITH LIFE,
a HOME THAT YOU
BELONG TO, a HOME
THAT CARRIES ALL
THERE EVER WAS AND EXISTS
IN THIS MOMENT.

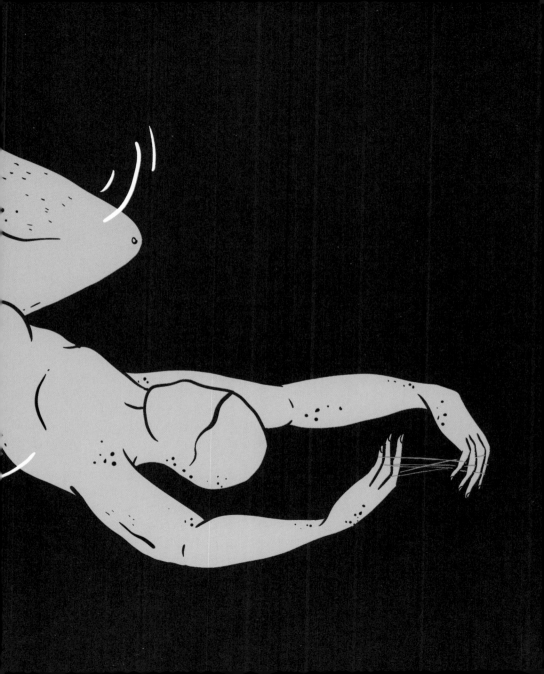

PLACE YOUR
HAND OVER YOUR HEART,
CLOSE YOUR EYES IF YOU CHOOSE,
AND CONNECT TO ALL THE LIFE
THAT'S FLOWING WITHIN YOU.

PLEASE KNOW
THESE PAGES ARE ALWAYS
HERE FOR you to RETURN to,
a PLACE WHERE you CAN
RECONNECT, REST IN THE
MIDDLE of THINGS,
AND FIND REFUGE
        IN yourSELF.

you ARE MEANT TO BE HERE

X

YOUR BODY IS
YOUR HOME

SECTION THREE

RESOURCES

MAKING a
HOME of YOURSELF
~~OFTEN~~ ALWAYS REQUIRES
ASKING FOR HELP:
FROM FRIENDS, FAMILY,
PETS, ~~YOURSELF~~, THE UNIVERSE,
AND PROFESSIONALS.

THERAPIES AND PRACTICES THAT HELP BUILD RESILIENCE

SOMATIC EXPERIENCING

HYPNOTHERAPY

ART THERAPY

EMDR (EYE MOVEMENT DESENSITIZATION AND REPROCESSING)

TRAUMA-INFORMED CBT (COGNITIVE BEHAVIORAL THERAPY)

ATTACHMENT PSYCHOTHERAPY

INTERNAL FAMILY SYSTEMS

DBT (DIALECTICAL BEHAVIORAL THERAPY)

SENSORIMOTOR PSYCHOTHERAPY

MINDFULNESS

MEDITATION

TRAUMA-INFORMED YOGA

ACUPUNCTURE

EMOTIONAL FREEDOM TECHNIQUE

AYURVEDIC MEDICINE

ENERGY HEALING

CRANIOSACRAL THERAPY

LIFE COACHING

MUSIC THERAPY

SOUND HEALING

MYOFASCIAL RELEASE

MOVEMENT

VISUALIZATION

ALEXANDER TECHNIQUE

REFLEXOLOGY

MASSAGE THERAPY

NATURE THERAPY

AROMATHERAPY

BIOFEEDBACK

NEUROFEEDBACK

HEALING TOUCH

HERE ARE SOME WAYS TO TEND TO YOURSELF

→

PHYSICAL

Take Naps

Hydrate

Take Your Meds

Stretch

Lie in the Grass

Schedule Regular Checkups with Your Doctor

Connect to Your Senses

Connect to Your Breath

Trust and Believe in the Sensations of Your Body

Eat Foods That Make You Feel Good

Wear Clothes That Make You Feel Empowered

MENTAL

Follow Your Curiosity

Check in with Your Inner Critic

Give Your Mind a Break by Focusing on Your Body

Follow Guided Meditations

Read Engaging Articles

Engage in Discussions

Spend Time Alone

Make Art

Rest Your Mind by Taking a Nap

Take a Break from Social Media

Learn a New Skill

Take on a Perspective Different from Your Own

SPIRITUAL

Practice Gratitude

Meditate/Pray

Create Your Own Personal Rituals

Read Texts That Are Sacred to You

Evaluate Your Beliefs

Spend Time in Nature

EMOTIONAL

Go to Therapy

Spend Time with Trees

Journal

Acknowledge Your Feelings

Honor Your No

Set Energetic Boundaries

Accept All Emotions as Information

Spend Time Doing Nothing

Practice Mindfulness and Gratitude

Allow Yourself to Make Mistakes

Be Honest About Your Needs + Wants

Connect with Your Inner Child

SOCIAL

Check in with Your Core People

Write Love Letters to Your Friends

Attend a Support Group

Host a Dinner Party

State Your Needs and Boundaries

Evaluate Your Relationships

WEIGHTED BLANKET FOR ANXIETY

SENSORY PUTTY FOR STRESS
PUTTY

MAGNESIUM FOR ANXIETY
M

O3
OMEGA-3 OIL FOR DEPRESSION

DRY BRUSHING FOR DISSOCIATION

PROBIOTICS FOR VAGUS NERVE

A FEW THINGS to HELP you SELF-KEEP

Vit B

Vit D

VITAMINS D + B FOR DEPRESSION

I WANT TO REJECT _____.

I WILL DO SO BY RELEASING _____

AND BY CALLING IN _____.

MY BODY IS NOT A SPACE of _____

IT IS A SPACE FOR _____. WHEN THE

FEAR of _____ COMES TO ME

I WILL RESPOND WITH _____ AND

TAKE THE TENDEREST of CARE BY _____.

_____

I WANT TO ATTRACT _____. I WILL

DO SO BY RELEASING _____

AND BY CALLING IN _____.

MY BODY IS A SPACE of _____,

I CLAIM _____ AS MY OWN.

I REFUSE TO ACCEPT _____.

I AM MY OWN, MY BODY IS MINE.

X _____

VICTORIA EMANUELA

They/Them

WRITER, MIND-BODY EDUCATOR, AND MEDITATION TEACHER. THEIR WORK EXISTS AT THE INTERSECTION of EMBODIED HEALING AND SOMATIC WRITING. VICTORIA'S TENDER AND ENCOURAGING WORDS CREATE SPACE FOR HUMANS to CHOOSE THEMSELVES A LITTLE MORE BOLDLY.

CAITLIN
METZ

she/her

a FEISTY INTROVERT, TENDER QUEER, ILLUSTRATOR, AND EDUCATOR. HER WORK EXISTS AT THE INTERSECTIONal IDENTITY, MENTAL HEALTH, AND COMMUNITY. CAITLIN'S EMOTIVE AND IMMEDIATE MARK-MAKING FOSTERS CONNECTION, MAKING THE WORLD a LITTLE LESS LONELY.

CAITLIN CREATING WITH YOU HAS BEEN THE MOST HEALING PART OF LIVING. MEETING YOU AND INTERTWINING OUR PRACTICES HAS CHANGED MY LIFE. I WILL NEVER STOP SCREAMING ABOUT IDEAS WITH YOU. YOU GET ME. I LOVE YOU DEEPLY.

DAVID YOU ARE MY BEST FRIEND, MY HEART, AND THE DEEPEST BOND I'VE EVER KNOWN. I LOVE YOU SO MUCH, IT'S INSANE. THANK YOU FOR ALWAYS SEEING ME, MAKING ME LAUGH, AND LOVING ME UNCONDITIONALLY.

MAMA MY FIRST HOME, OLDEST FRIEND, AND NUMBER ONE FAN; YOUR INCREDIBLE LOVE KEEPS ME GOING. THANK YOU FOR YOUR UNCONDITIONAL SUPPORT, NEVER GIVING UP ON ME, AND GIVING ME MY CREATIVE FIRE. I LOVE YOU SO MUCH.

DADDY I WISH YOU WERE STILL HERE SO YOUR HANDS COULD HOLD THIS BOOK. THANK YOU FOR INSTILLING IN ME THE DEEPEST DRIVE TO CHASE AFTER MY DREAMS. I LOVE YOU AND MISS YOU EVERY DAY, BUT I KNOW YOU'RE STILL WITH ME.

SARA YOU WEREN'T JUST AN EDITOR BUT A FRIEND WHO CHEERED US ON, SHARED OUR TEARS, AND STOOD BY OUR SIDE. THANK YOU FOR SEEING US, OUR VISION AND MAKING OUR DREAMS COME TRUE.

CHRISTINE YOU SAW MY ABILITIES AND POTENTIAL WHEN I COULDN'T SEE MYSELF. THANK YOU FOR EVERY WORD OF LOVE AND ENCOURAGEMENT. THEY HAVE STAYED WITH ME AND KEEP ME GOING.

MY FUR-BABIES YOU HAVE BEEN THERE THROUGH EVERYTHING. YOU'VE GIVEN ME A REASON TO SMILE DURING MY DARKEST DAYS. THANK YOU FOR LOVING ME AND LETTING ME BE YOUR HUMXN. I'M BETTER BECAUSE OF YOU.

MY CHOSEN FAMILY AND FRIENDS YOUR LOVE AND ABILITY TO SEE ME FOR WHO I AM HAS HELPED ME LOVE MYSELF IN WAYS I THOUGHT WEREN'T POSSIBLE. YOU MEAN SO MUCH TO ME, AND ALWAYS WILL; I LOVE YOU.

love,
VICTORIA

SARA (OUR EDITOR)
OUR CHEERLEADER,
BELIEVER and GUIDE.

CYNTHIA (MY THERAPIST)
THE TRUE and UNSUNG HERO
of MY LIFE.

VICTORIA (♥)
THE COMPLETION of MY THOUGHTS,
THE FULLNESS of MY HEART.

ANDREW (MY PARTNER)
MY SOFTEST LANDING, and
STRONGEST FOUNDATION.

PENELOPE (THE SWEETEST PUP)
MY SNUGGLIEST, TENDEREST,
FOREVER BY MY SIDE, LOVE.

love,
CAITLIN

GOODBYE
DARLINGS